PRESENTED TO:

....

FROM:

....

DATE:

....

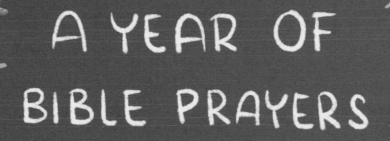

A YEAR OF
BIBLE PRAYERS

A TREASURY OF 48 PRAYER
STORIES FROM GOD'S WORD

written by Jo Anne Simmons

illustrated by Anita Schmidt

BARBOUR kidz

A Division of Barbour Publishing

ISBN 978-1-63609-481-6

Published by Barbour Publishing, Inc., 1810 Barbour Drive, Uhrichsville, Ohio 44683, www.barbourbooks.com

Our mission is to inspire the world with the life-changing message of the Bible.

 Member of the
Evangelical Christian
Publishers Association

Printed in China.

001449 0123 HA

CONTENTS

JANUARY

Prayers for Protection

The world is full of good things that give us fun and joy and giggles. The world also has some sad and scary things that make us worry and cry and feel afraid. But above all of these things stands our great big God. Can you picture Him? He's watching over you with love every moment of every day, in the good times and the bad. He knows, He cares, He provides, and He protects—not always the way you want or expect Him to, but always in the ways that are best. Throughout the Bible, we see time and again how people prayed to God for help and protection from the sad and scary things of life. These examples help us remember to pray for God's help and protection too. Read the following stories this month and see for yourself!

"THIS NATION IS YOUR PEOPLE"

Moses' Prayer for God's Presence to Go with Israel to Canaan

Back in ancient Bible times, the baby who floated down the Nile River in a basket grew up to be the man God chose to lead His people, the Israelites, out of slavery in Egypt. That man was Moses, and God talked to Moses just like a friend.

God instructed Moses to lead the people for forty years in the wilderness as He worked out His good plans for them. He showed them miraculous things like parting the Red Sea so they could walk right through. He used a pillar of cloud to lead them during the day and a pillar of fire to lead them by night. He gave them meat to eat each night. And He gave them bread, called manna, which rained down from heaven every morning. But even as God took such good care of them, sometimes the Israelites didn't like what God was doing and the places where He was leading. Sometimes they grumbled and complained. They were impatient and rude and made bad choices. They even melted down all their golden earrings to create a false god to worship instead of the one true God.

That was a big mistake, and God became very angry—angry enough that He told them He would no longer be with them to help them and protect them. But God's anger never kept Him from loving them. He still let Moses talk to Him on their behalf. Moses pleaded with God not to leave the Israelites alone. He said, "This nation is Your people. Don't let us leave this place without You." Moses knew they would all be lost and in great danger if God was not with them. The people needed God to be present in their lives to guide and protect them.

God was pleased with Moses. He listened with compassion to Moses' prayer for help, and He answered, "I Myself will go with you. I will give you rest." God loves His people no matter what, and God hears and answers honest, humble prayers for His help and His presence and His protection.

(Adapted from Exodus 2; 13–14; 31–33)

"LORD, SAVE ME!"
Peter's Prayer to Be Saved from Drowning

Jesus loved His friends, the disciples, and He loved all the people who came to Him to learn and to be healed. But sometimes He needed quiet time alone to rest and pray to God the Father.

One day, after His miracle of turning five small loaves of bread and two fish into a lunch big enough to feed more than five thousand people, Jesus told His disciples to get in their boat and go on ahead. He was headed up the mountain alone for time to talk to God the Father.

Later that night, the disciples in the boat found themselves tossed around in the middle of a storm. The wind and the waves were strong and wild. And just before dawn, they looked out on the water and froze, suddenly very afraid. "It's a ghost!" they cried.

But it wasn't a ghost at all. It was Jesus! "Don't be afraid," He told them. "It's Me!"

Jesus' friend Peter was very bold and brave, and he loved Jesus very much. He said, "Lord, if it's You, tell me to walk out to You on the water."

And Jesus said, "Come on, then!"

So Peter got out of the boat and took one step—and then another! He was walking on water just like Jesus!

Before long, though, Peter noticed the strong wind. He surely felt those wild waves. He grew very afraid, and he started to sink. "Lord, save me!" he cried out to Jesus.

And right away, Jesus grabbed Peter by the hand, and Peter was safe.

Jesus said to Peter, "You have so little faith! Why did you doubt?"

Then Jesus and Peter got into the boat, and the storm quickly stopped.

Everyone in the boat worshipped Jesus and told Him, "You are the Son of God!"

Jesus loves when people are full of strong faith and courage, yet He knows that sometimes our faith and courage grow weak. But when people cry out to Him, "Lord, save me!" He reaches out to answer that prayer with great big love and exactly the help that we need.

(Adapted from Matthew 14)

"OPEN HIS EYES, THAT HE MIGHT SEE"

Elisha's Prayer for His Servant's Understanding

When the nation of Syria was fighting against God's nation of Israel, the prophet Elisha, who spoke for God, was helping the Israelites and warning them of danger. God gave Elisha the power to know what the Syrian king was saying and the moves he would make. So Elisha helped protect the Israelites by telling them where to go to avoid being killed and defeated in battle.

The king of Syria was very angry because of this. He called his servants and said to them, "Show me which one of us is helping the king of Israel!" He thought there must be a traitor among them.

But one of his men told him about Elisha being a prophet of God. "None of us is a traitor, O king," the man said. "Elisha tells the king of Israel the very words you say in your bedroom."

So the king of Syria said, "Go and see where Elisha is." And he soon sent an army of many soldiers to find and capture the man of God. They snuck in at night and gathered around the city where Elisha was staying.

Early in the morning Elisha's servant went out and saw the enemy army ready to capture Elisha. "This is really bad!" he told Elisha. "What should we do?"

"Don't be afraid," Elisha said to his servant, "for those who are with us are more than those who are with them." And then he prayed, "O Lord, open his eyes, that he might see."

And God opened the eyes of Elisha's servant and showed him that the mountain around them was full of horses and chariots of fire. They were ready to protect and fight for God's people of Israel!

Then Elisha prayed that the enemy army would be blinded so that he could lead them unaware to another city—right where the armies of Israel could capture them. And when God opened their eyes again, they realized where they were. But Elisha told the king of Israel to be kind to them. So the king fed them a meal and sent them away.

God's people today might often feel outnumbered by enemies, but we can call on Him—anytime, anywhere—to open our eyes so that we might see the miraculous ways He loves us and fights for us and protects us.

(Adapted from 2 Kings 6)

"NOT WHAT I WANT BUT WHAT YOU WANT"

Jesus' Prayer to Avoid the Suffering of the Cross

When the time was drawing near for Jesus to suffer and die on the cross, He needed to pray to God the Father. He went to a garden called Gethsemane with three of His disciples. He said to them, "My soul is very sad. Please stay here with Me, keep watch with Me, and pray with Me."

Then He went a little farther into the garden and got down with His face on the ground. He prayed to ask God the Father—if there was any way to do it—to please protect Him and take away the suffering that He knew was about to happen with His death on the cross. "But," He added, "not what I want but what You want."

Then He went back to His three friends and found that they were asleep. That upset Him. "Couldn't you watch and pray with Me for just one hour?" He asked them. He needed encouragement, but His friends had let Him down. So He asked them again to watch and pray—and stay awake this time!

Again He went alone to pray to God, saying, "My Father, if this must happen to Me, may whatever You want be done." And then He went back to His friends and found them sleeping again. So He went away from them a third time and prayed to God the same prayer—"Not what I want but what You want."

Finally, Jesus went back to His sleepy friends and told them to get up because it would soon be time for God's plans for Him to unfold. The Father's will would be done.

Jesus is our perfect hero and example. We can pray for protection from suffering, just like He did. But even more importantly, just like Jesus, we should pray for what God wants to be done—even if it's very different from what we want. Through Jesus' suffering and death and rising to life again, God was working to save people. And in whatever suffering we must go through, God is working out His perfect plans too.

(Adapted from Matthew 26)

FEBRUARY

Prayers of Love and Blessing

February makes us think of Valentine's Day, and Valentine's Day makes us think of love! And love should make us think of God because if not for Him, we wouldn't know how to love at all. He created love. The Bible says God *is* love. Think of the people who love and bless you in your life, like your mom or dad, grandpa or grandma, brother or sister, and your favorite teachers, coaches, and babysitters. The Bible says if those people know how wonderful it is to love you and give you good blessings, then you should think of how much more God, your heavenly Father who created you, must want to love and bless you. It's oodles and *oodles* more! As you are filled with love and blessings from the people who love you and the one true God who loves you, you should want that love and blessing to overflow out of you and onto others. Do you pray for love and blessings for others? People in Bible times did. Jesus did too. And we can learn from them. Read the following stories this month and see for yourself!

"LET HER BE THE ONE"

Eliezer's Prayer to Find a Wife for Isaac

Isaac was the son born to Abraham and Sarah after they thought they were far too old to have children. But God promised they would have a son, and God's promises are always true. One day, after Isaac was all grown up, Abraham said to his servant Eliezer, "Go to my home country, and the people I grew up with, to find a bride for Isaac."

But Eliezer had a question. "What if the woman doesn't want to follow me back here to this land? Shouldn't I take your son with me to the land where you came from?"

Abraham insisted he should not. "God promised me: 'I will give this land to your children and to their children's children.' He will send His angel in front of you to help make sure you can find a bride for my son from there."

So Eliezer loaded ten camels with lots of supplies and lots of gifts, and he set off to a place called Nahor to find a bride for Isaac. It was a long journey, and by the time Eliezer and the ten camels finally arrived, they were tired. And hot. And very thirsty. They stopped outside the city near a well of water in the evening, and Eliezer let the camels get down on their knees to rest. Then he asked God to show him who should be Isaac's wife. He prayed, "O Lord, here by the well, I can watch the daughters of the men of the city come get water. If I say to a girl, 'Could you let me drink a little water from your jar, please?' and she answers, 'Drink, and I will give water to your camels also,' let her be the one You have chosen to be Isaac's wife." And before he had even finished praying, a beautiful young woman named Rebekah came out to the well with a water jar on her shoulder.

"Could you let me drink a little water from your jar, please?" Eliezer asked her.

"Yes," she said. "Drink." And she gave him her water jar. Then she said, "And I will get water for your camels also." And she did.

Eliezer thought, *She must be the one!* God had answered his prayer so quickly! He soon met Rebekah's family. He told them how he had prayed and how God answered that prayer through Rebekah when she gave both him and his camels water. He said, "I bowed low and worshipped. I gave honor and thanks to the Lord, the God of my boss, Abraham. For God led me in the right way."

And Rebekah's father and brother answered, "This is surely from the Lord. Take Rebekah to be the wife of your boss's son."

God was pleased that Eliezer wanted to bless Abraham by bringing home the right bride for Isaac. Eliezer's name means "God is my help," and God surely showed His help to Eliezer and His blessing to Abraham and Isaac through Rebekah.

(Adapted from Genesis 24)

"KEEP THEM IN THE POWER OF YOUR NAME"
Jesus' Prayer for His Followers

When Jesus lived on earth, He traveled and taught and preached. He made friends and enemies. He camped under the stars. He walked on water and calmed stormy seas. He healed people who were blind and deaf and sick. He brought dead people back to life. He turned a little bit of food into a great big picnic lunch! And He blessed and loved and cared for all the people. On top of these many things, Jesus prayed for people too.

One day after He had been preaching and teaching, He began to pray for His friends, the disciples. Jesus prayed to His Father in heaven, saying, "I have made Your name known to My friends. You gave them to Me. They have obeyed Your Word. Now they know that everything You have given Me came from You. I gave them the Word, and they received it. They know I came from You, and they believe You sent Me."

Then He prayed for God to bless His friends and keep them in the power of God's name after Jesus joined His Father in heaven. "I am coming to You," He prayed, "but these friends are still in the world. Holy Father, keep them in the power of Your name. Then they will be one, even as We are one."

And finally, He prayed for His disciples, saying, "Keep them from the devil. My followers do not belong to the world, just as I do not belong to the world. Make them holy by Your Word, which is truth. You sent Me into the world, and I have sent them into the world."

And then Jesus prayed for all of His friends and followers in the future too—including me, including you! He said, "I pray for those who will put their trust in Me through the teaching they have heard. May they be united, Father, just like You are in Me and I am in You. May they belong to Us. Then the world will believe that You sent Me and that You love them as You love Me."

(Adapted from John 17)

"REMEMBER ME FOR THIS, GOD"
Nehemiah's Prayer for Blessing

Nehemiah was a Jewish man who lived in ancient Bible times. He served as the cupbearer for the king of Persia. Cupbearers had a serious job—the job of tasting all the king's food and drink before the king did. That way, the cupbearer could make sure no one was trying to poison the king!

One day Nehemiah looked sad, and the king noticed. He said, "Why is your face so sad when you are not sick, Nehemiah? Are you sad in your heart?"

Nehemiah replied, "How can my face not be sad when my family's city is in ruins?"

So the king said, "What is it you are asking for?"

Nehemiah replied, "If it pleases you, and if you approve, send me to Jerusalem. Let me build the city again."

The king liked Nehemiah and had been pleased with his work, so he gave Nehemiah permission to go. Nehemiah soon got a group of good builders together, and within fifty-two days, they rebuilt the city of Jerusalem's walls! It was a great big job in a short amount of time, and it showed God's great big power was at work in His people. Nehemiah loved and respected God with all his heart, and he continued to help the Jewish people honor and obey God in all things.

At the end of his life, Nehemiah thought back over the good deeds he had done—the ways he helped the Jewish people follow God. He said, "I went to Jerusalem and learned about the sinful things done to the house of God. I was very angry. I said, 'Why is the house of God no longer cared for?'" Nehemiah had helped the people correct their

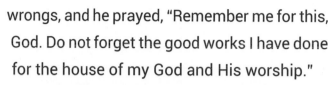

wrongs, and he prayed, "Remember me for this, God. Do not forget the good works I have done for the house of my God and His worship."

And as he thought back over more good deeds from his life—like how he helped the Jewish people follow God's commands—he prayed again. "Remember me for this also, God. Be good to me because You are loving."

Nehemiah reminds us that our good deeds for God matter. When we love and serve Him faithfully and inspire others to follow His ways, we can ask God to remember what we have done and bless us too!

(Adapted from Nehemiah 1–6; 13)

"WELL IN EVERY WAY"
John's Prayer that Gaius Would Prosper

Jesus had twelve disciples, and two of them were brothers named James and John. Jesus called them the Sons of Thunder! They were bold and brave and eager as they followed Jesus and learned from Him. One day when the people of a town called Samaria did not want to welcome Jesus into the town, James and John asked Him, "Jesus, do You want us to call down fire from heaven to burn the town up?" Jesus had to settle them down.

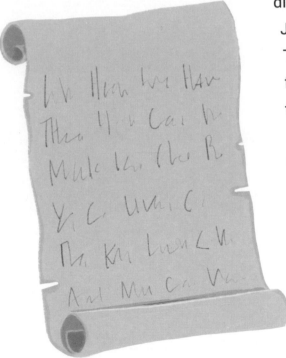

When Jesus was dying on the cross, John was the disciple He asked to look after His mother, Mary. Jesus said to Mary, "Woman, look at your son." Then He said to John, "Look at your mother." And from then on, Mary lived with John, and he cared for her as if she really was his mother.

Later in his life, John was a busy writer. He wrote five books of the Bible! He wrote the Gospel of John to describe the life and work of Jesus. He wrote the book of Revelation to record his visions about the last days of this world. And he wrote three letters called 1 John, 2 John, and 3 John.

In the first of these letters, John wrote to make sure the Christians then and the

Christians now would know that Jesus was a real man, and He was also really God—and that He loves people so much. In the second letter, John wrote to warn people against false teachers. And in the third letter, John wrote to his friend Gaius to encourage him to always do what is good and not do what is evil. Gaius was faithful to God and to others, and he was kind and welcoming to strangers. He was known for his love and for walking in truth.

John wrote to Gaius in his letter, "I love you, dear friend. I pray that you are doing well in every way. I pray that your body and soul are strong and well."

Who are the loved ones and friends you pray for like that? Whose body and soul do you want to be strong and well in every way? Pray blessings on them just like Jesus' friend John did for his friend Gaius!

(Adapted from Mark 3; Luke 9; John 19; 3 John)

Prayers for Healing

When winter turns to spring, we see beautiful new life. The frozen ground thaws out and welcomes new seeds to get cozy so that they can take root and grow. Plants and flowers and trees that were huddled in tight to survive the cold get nourished by the sunshine and warmer weather, and they begin to emerge and bloom again. The change from winter to spring is wonderful! Many people in Bible times needed help changing too. They had illness and injury and trouble that hurt and held them back. But God has all power to heal and make new, and we see that over and over in the pages of the Bible. Through the accounts of healing recorded in the Bible, we can be inspired to pray for healing for both others and ourselves. Read the following stories this month and see for yourself!

~~ "TAKE PITY ON US, SON OF DAVID" ~~
Two Men's Prayer for Healing from Blindness

No matter the weather or time of day, no matter if the sun shone bright or if the skies were gray, two men back in Bible times lived in total darkness They were blind and could not see. And their blindness made their lives hard.

But even though they did not have sight, the two men had hope! They knew of old prophecies that told of a Messiah. This Savior would be from the Jewish family line of David. The book of Isaiah said that He would help those who are blind see and make people happier.

Another prophecy from Isaiah said, "The eyes of people who are blind will be opened. And the ears of those who can't hear will be opened. And those who can't walk will jump like a deer. And those who can't speak will call out for joy."

And yet another one said, "He will open blind eyes. He will bring people out of the prison of darkness."

So when the two men who were blind heard about a man named Jesus who was teaching and preaching and healing people, they wondered, *Could He be the Messiah we've hoped for and dreamed about? Could He fulfill the old prophecies? Could He heal us? Could He make us see?*

Imagine their excitement when they realized Jesus was traveling by their area! "Let's follow Him," they said. And they did. And they cried out to Him, "Take pity on us, Son of David." They even followed Jesus into someone's house. They had to use their senses of hearing and touch to get around carefully, since they couldn't see.

Jesus said to them, "Do you have faith that I can do this?"

"Yes, sir!" they said to Him.

Then Jesus put His hands on their eyes and said, "You will have what you want because of your faith."

And suddenly, their eyes were opened. They could see! Light and colors, people and buildings, trees and birds. . .*everything*! And it was all so beautiful to the two men who once were blind but now could see. The two men were excited! They told everyone they could about Jesus, and news about Him spread all over their country.

God can still heal people. So when you know someone is sick, ask Him to help them get better. He might make them just as happy as the men who were once blind.

(Adapted from Isaiah 29; 35; 42; Matthew 9)

~~ "PLEASE PUT YOUR HAND ON HIM" ~~
A Prayer for a Man Who Couldn't Hear or Speak

He could see, but he could not hear. He could feel, but he could barely talk. What must life have been like for a man who was deaf and couldn't speak back in ancient Bible times? Was he lonely? Did he have a family? Could he work a job? What were his friends like?

The man clearly had people who cared about him because when Jesus traveled back to the Sea of Galilee, those friends brought him to Jesus. They had heard that Jesus could do great miracles—He could heal people who had disabilities and people who were sick and people who were blind. Surely He could heal someone who was deaf and who couldn't speak!

"Please put Your hand on him," the man's friends begged Jesus.

Jesus must have wanted some space. He took the man a bit away from the other people. He put his fingers into the man's ears. Then Jesus spit on His own finger and put it on the man's tongue. Next, Jesus looked up to heaven and breathed deeply from within. "Be opened!" He said.

At once the man's ears were opened! He was no longer deaf! He could hear everything! At once the man's tongue was made loose! He could now speak just like other people! What sounds did he notice first? Did he hear the gasps and happy cries of his friends who had just witnessed the miracle of his healing? What words did he use right away? Did he say a great big "Thank You!" to Jesus?

Jesus told the people there that they shouldn't tell anyone about the miracle. But the more He told people this, the more they talked about what He had done. They were very

surprised and wondered why they should keep Jesus' miracles a secret. They said, "He has done all things well. He helps people hear. He helps people speak."

"Please put Your hand on him," the man's friends had begged of Jesus. We can beg Jesus to put His hand on us and our loved ones today too. We can trust that He always does all things well.

(Adapted from Mark 7)

"LORD, YOU CAN HEAL ME!"
A Man's Prayer for Healing from Leprosy

Itchy, scabby spots and sores—*ewww*—no one wants those! But many people in Bible times suffered from skin diseases and needed healing. And there were not hospitals and clinics and doctors all around. Leprosy was a well-known skin disease—and it was terrible. People who had it were avoided by others who feared catching it. Sometimes these people were banished from their homes and towns and cities and sent to live in caves along with other people who had leprosy. It was rare that anyone wanted to help them. No one knew how to cure and heal leprosy.

No one but Jesus. He knew how to cure and heal, and He was not afraid of skin diseases.

One day Jesus came down from a mountainside, and large crowds of people followed Him. Soon a man with leprosy came to Jesus and got down on his knees before Jesus to worship Him. The man said, "Lord, if You will, You can heal me!"

And Jesus put His hand on him and said, "I will. You are healed!"

At once the man was healed. No more scabs or spots or sores!

Jesus could have simply said the words, "You're

healed." He didn't have to place His hand on the man with leprosy. But He did. Jesus showed great compassion and care to a man no one else would touch or even go near.

Jesus said to the man, "Go now, but tell no one. Let the religious leader see you. This will show them you have been healed." The law in those days said people who had been healed of leprosy had to be examined by a religious leader to be declared clean. Only then could they return to their home and neighbors. How clean and fresh and new the man healed of leprosy must have felt! How happy he must have been to get to see people up close again.

Jesus comes to those who need healing and help. He gives them great love and care and is willing to touch and restore those who have faith in Him. In any illness or injury, always remember that Jesus alone is worthy of the prayer, "Lord, You can heal me!"

(Adapted from Matthew 8)

"O GOD, HEAL HER, I PRAY!"
Moses' Prayer for Miriam

Brothers and sisters don't always get along well. They fight and argue sometimes. That was just as common in Bible times as it is today. One day Moses and his brother, Aaron, and their sister, Miriam, were in the middle of an argument. They weren't kids anymore either. They were all grown up! Aaron and Miriam spoke against Moses because they disagreed about the woman he'd chosen to marry. And then they were full of pride, saying, "Is it true that the Lord has spoken *only* through Moses? Has He not spoken through us also?"

God hears everything, and He heard them. And God knows everything too. They couldn't hide their pride from God. But Moses was a man with no pride. He was not full of a bragging, better-than-everyone-else attitude. He thought of others more than himself. He was the humblest man on earth. And when God heard the prideful things that Aaron and Miriam were saying, He said to Moses and Aaron and Miriam, "You three come out to the meeting tent."

So the three of them went out. Then the Lord came down in a cloud and stood at the door of the meeting tent. He called to Aaron and Miriam. When both of them came near, God said, "Now listen to Me. My servant Moses is faithful in all My house. He is the only one I speak with face-to-face. And he is the only one who sees what the Lord is like. So why weren't you afraid to speak against My servant Moses?"

God was angry with them, and He left. And when the cloud lifted from over the meeting tent, Miriam had leprosy—that very bad skin disease. It turned her skin as white as snow! Everyone would be afraid to catch it from her. Would they run away from her? Would she die from the leprosy?

Even though the siblings had quarreled, they loved one another, and Aaron was scared for his sister. He saw her skin disease and said to Moses, "Oh, I beg you. We don't want to be punished because we have been foolish and have sinned. Don't let Miriam suffer with this skin disease!"

Moses knew the matter was in God's hands. He cried out to the Lord, saying, "O God, heal her, I pray!"

And God listened to Moses. He had mercy on Miriam because of her brother's prayer.

(Adapted from Numbers 12)

APRIL

Prayers to Bring the Dead Back to Life

Death isn't fun to think about. Anyone who has ever lost a family member or friend knows how sad it is. It's hard to lose someone you love so much and have to learn to live without them. But even though death is sad and scary, God has the superpower over it! And Eastertime is when we celebrate that. God alone can bring people back from death to life. And because His Son, Jesus, took our sin when He died on the cross and was raised to life again, you can trust that you will also rise to life again after death if you admit your sin and believe in Jesus as your Savior. Have you done that so you will live forever? Pray to God and let Him give you that gift. Have all your family and friends done that so they will live forever? Pray for them to trust Jesus as Savior and receive new life too. Meanwhile, keep loving God well as you live here on earth. Ask Him to show you the good things He created you for. Keep learning about God through His Word, and let the Bible remind you that God alone has the power to bring the dead back to life. Read the following stories this month and see for yourself!

"FATHER, I THANK YOU FOR HEARING ME"

Jesus' Prayer for the Resurrection of Lazarus

When Jesus lived on earth, three of His dearest friends were Mary, Martha, and Lazarus. They were siblings who lived together in a town called Bethany. When Lazarus became very ill, Mary and Martha were scared for their brother. They knew he might die. So they sent word to Jesus, who was traveling. When Jesus heard his friend Lazarus was sick, He stayed two more days where He was but then said to His disciples, "Let's go into the country of Judea again." That's where Bethany was.

The disciples were afraid for Jesus because people in Judea had tried to kill Him. They said, "Teacher, the Jews tried to throw stones at You to kill You there not long ago. Are you really going to Judea again?"

Jesus said that He was. As He traveled, He learned that Lazarus had died and been buried.

The grave where Lazarus was buried was a hole in the side of a hill. A stone covered the door. When Jesus got there, He said, "Take the stone away." But Martha said to Him, "Lord, by now his body has a bad smell. He has been dead four days."

And Jesus said to her, "Did I not say that if you would believe you would see the greatness of God?"

So they took the stone away. Jesus looked up and said, "Father, I thank You for hearing Me. I know You always hear Me. But I said that so the people standing here would believe

You have sent Me." Then He called with a loud voice, "Lazarus, come out!"

And Lazarus did! His hands and feet and face and body were all tied up and covered in graveclothes, so Jesus said to the people, "Take off the graveclothes and let him go." The man who had been dead for four days was alive and well again!

Jesus had told Martha, "Your brother will rise again. I am the one who raises the dead and gives them life. Anyone who trusts in Me will live again and never die. Do you believe

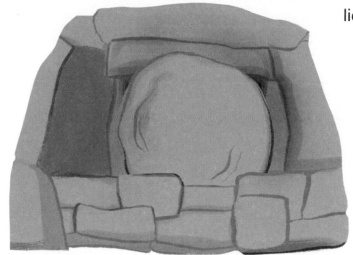

this?" Martha answered, "Yes, Lord, I believe that You are the Christ, the Son of God, who has come into the world." Jesus proved Himself true when He raised Lazarus from the dead. And we prove ourselves faithful to Jesus today by continuing to believe in Jesus like Martha did.

(Adapted from John 11)

"GET UP, TABITHA!"

Peter's Prayer for Tabitha's Resurrection

A woman named Tabitha was a follower of Jesus. She lived in the town of Joppa and was known for being good and kind and making lovely clothing for others to wear—beautiful tunics and other things that were stylish back then. When she became sick and then died, her friends were very sad. They had loved her so much and had appreciated how giving she was to others.

Tabitha's friends washed and prepared her body, in the customs of their day, and laid her in a room on the second floor of a house. But even though she had died, her friends still had hope. They knew of a special man who also loved and followed Jesus—a man named Peter. He had been Jesus' disciple not that long ago when Jesus lived on earth. This was the same Peter who had asked Jesus to help him walk on water! And now Peter was known to heal the sick and raise the dead back to life in Jesus' name.

Tabitha's friends had heard Peter was traveling through a town nearby. So two of Tabitha's friends went to Peter and begged him to come and help Tabitha. "Hurry, please!" they urged him. "Our dear friend has died, but we have heard of you, and we believe you can help."

Peter agreed to come with them, and he went to the house where they had laid Tabitha's body. Her friends were gathered around her, weeping and crying, for they missed their dear friend. They showed Peter all the nice clothing she had made them.

Then Peter told them to leave the room, and he kneeled and prayed to God. Peter was full of faith. He had seen with his own eyes the many miracles of Jesus, and he

prayed to God knowing that all miracles come from Him.

Then he said to Tabitha, "Get up, Tabitha!" And she opened her eyes and looked at Peter and sat up! He took her by the hand and helped her get up. Then he presented her to all her friends and the people gathered there to show them God had raised Tabitha from death to life. Imagine how happy they were! Imagine how they must have hugged and kissed her. Imagine how their tears of sadness turned to tears of joy. After all the excitement, Tabitha probably went right back to doing the many good and kind things she loved to do.

News of Tabitha being brought back to life spread throughout Joppa. And because of that incredible news, many people put their trust in Jesus. Have you put your trust in Him? If not, He would love to be part of your life!

(Adapted from Acts 9)

"LET THIS CHILD'S LIFE RETURN TO HIM"

Elijah's Prayer for the Resurrection of the Widow's Son

The prophet Elijah spoke messages from God. One day he warned King Ahab, "There will be no rain for the next few years." Without water, plants and food would not grow, and animals and people would die.

Ahab was a very bad king who did not honor God, and he did not like this warning. So God told Elijah, "Leave here and hide from King Ahab by the river. Drink from the river. I have told the ravens to bring you food to eat."

Elijah obeyed. He had food and water just as God promised. But after a while, the river dried up because there was no rain in the land.

Then God told Elijah, "Go to the town called Zarephath. I have told a woman there to feed you." Again, Elijah obeyed. When he came to the city, he saw a woman gathering sticks. He said, "Could you get me a little water in a jar so I can have a drink?" She agreed, and then Elijah asked, "Could you also bring me a piece of bread to eat?"

But to that she said, "I have no bread—only a little flour and oil. See, I am gathering sticks to bake something small for me and my son so we won't starve."

Elijah said, "Don't be afraid. Go and do as you have said. But make me a little loaf of bread first. For God says, 'The jar of flour will not be used up. The jar of oil will not be empty, until the day the Lord sends rain down on the earth.'"

So the woman did what Elijah said. And she and her son and Elijah ate for many days! The jar of flour was not used up, and the jar of oil did not become empty. It happened just like God had said.

Before long, though, the woman's son grew sick and died. She cried and was angry. But Elijah said, "Give me your son." He carried the boy to a bedroom, laid him down on a bed, and prayed, "O Lord, let this child's life return to him." God listened. The child came back to life and became strong again! Imagine how his mother must have celebrated!

She knew that God was real and His Word was true. From her story, and from the work of God in our own lives, we can believe that too.

(Adapted from 1 Kings 17)

"LORD, REMEMBER HOW I HAVE WALKED WITH YOU"
Hezekiah's Prayer for a Longer Life

Hezekiah was a king of Judah who did what was good and right and true. He wanted to obey God with his whole heart. Because of that, all went well for Hezekiah.

But even good people can still get sick. One day Hezekiah got very sick. The prophet Isaiah came to him and said, "This is what the Lord says: 'Get those of your house ready. For you will die. You will not get well again.'"

But Hezekiah had hope. He knew he could still ask God to give him a longer life. He turned his face to the wall and prayed, "Lord, remember how I have walked with You in truth and with my whole heart. I have done what is good in Your eyes." Then Hezekiah began to cry.

God was listening to Hezekiah. The Lord heard his cries and saw his tears. So before Isaiah had even left the room, God told him, "Tell Hezekiah, 'This is what the Lord says: "I have heard your prayer. I have seen your tears. And I will heal you. On the third day you must go up to the house of the Lord. And I will add fifteen years to your life."'"

Then Isaiah said to the king's servants, "Get some figs and make them into a loaf. Lay that loaf on the sore on Hezekiah's body. Then he will be well again." They did, and Hezekiah was healed! God answered Hezekiah's prayer for a longer life.

Hezekiah then asked Isaiah how he would know that he was truly healed when he went to the temple as God had instructed. He asked, "What will be the special thing for me to see?"

Isaiah answered, "The special thing for you to see is up to you. Would you like the sun's shadow to go ten steps farther or to go back ten steps?"

Hezekiah replied, "It's easy for the shadow to go ten steps farther. Let the shadow turn back ten steps." So Isaiah asked God to change the shadows as a sign for Hezekiah, and God did!

God heard and answered Hezekiah's prayer for new life. God heard and answered Isaiah's prayer for a sign for Hezekiah. God hears and answers our prayers today, too, especially when we walk with Him in truth and serve Him with our whole hearts.

(Adapted from 2 Kings 20)

MAY

Prayers of Mothers

In May, the month of Mother's Day, we honor and celebrate our moms and those who are like mothers to us. We give them presents and make them treats; we hug them tight and kiss their cheeks! We let them know what a blessing they are to us and tell them all the things we appreciate about them. We should especially appreciate a mom who prays! A loving mom who prays for her children is an extra-special treasure. Her prayers are so heartfelt and important. She wants the very best for her children, and she prays to God to ask for His blessings and protection and good gifts for them. She loves to take care of her children, but she knows that sometimes she can't. She also knows that it's really *God* who takes care of them in all things. We can learn from what God's Word shares with us about Bible-time mothers and their prayers for their children. Read the following stories this month and see for yourself!

"DON'T FORGET ME!"
Hannah's Prayer for a Son

A woman named Hannah, who lived in ancient Bible times, really wanted to be a mother. But she and her husband had no children together. She cried and prayed, asking God to let her have a baby boy. She felt so heartbroken and jealous when she saw other women having children. Sometimes she felt like God had forgotten her or didn't care about her. Her husband would say to her, "Hannah, why are you crying and not eating? And why is your heart sad? Am I not better to you than ten sons?"

But still Hannah kept praying. "Don't forget me, God!" she said. "Look at how troubled and sad I am, and please give me a son." She even made Him a big, important promise, saying, "If You give me a son, I will give him back to You for all the days of his life." She meant that if God gave her a son, then she would let her son live at the temple to grow up and be a servant of God.

One day, a religious leader named Eli was sitting at the door of the temple, and he watched Hannah. He could see Hannah's lips moving, but she made no sounds. At first, he didn't understand what she was doing or what was wrong with her. He thought she might have been drinking. "Put away the wine!" he told her.

"No, I'm not drunk!" Hannah told Eli. "I am troubled in my spirit. I was speaking to the Lord quietly in my heart."

Then Eli said, "Go in peace, and may the God of Israel give you what you asked Him for."

Right away, Hannah felt much better. Her face was no longer sad. She went home with her husband, and soon she did have a baby boy! She named him Samuel, saying, "I asked the Lord for him."

Sometimes, like Hannah, we might feel as though God has forgotten us. But that is never true. He knows us and remembers us. He loves us and listens to our prayers.

(Adapted from 1 Samuel 1)

～ "MY HEART IS HAPPY IN THE LORD!" ～
Hannah's Prayer of Gratitude

Hannah loved baby Samuel so much, and she took good care of him. But she never forgot her prayers and her promise to God. When the little boy was old enough, Hannah went back to the temple where she had met Eli. She said to Eli, "I am the woman you saw praying to the Lord. I asked for my son, and God gave him to me. So now I give him back to God for his whole life." She was letting Samuel live at the temple, where Eli would take care of him. There, Samuel would grow up and be a servant of God.

It was not easy for Hannah to leave Samuel at the temple. She would miss him living at home. Still, Hannah was grateful to God for answering her prayer and blessing her with a son. So she prayed, "My heart is happy in the Lord! My mouth speaks against those who hate me. I have joy in the Lord's saving power. There is no one holy like the Lord. For sure, there is no one better."

She went on to pray more powerful words, saying, "The Lord is a God who knows. He weighs our actions. He kills and brings to life. He raises people from the dead. The Lord makes people poor and rich. But He lifts the poor from the dust. And He lifts those in need from the ashes. He gives them a seat of honor next to rulers. He created the world, and He watches over it and His good people. Those who fight against the Lord will not win. He will give power to His chosen one."

Every year, Hannah came back to the temple to visit Samuel. And God blessed Hannah with three more sons and two daughters. She was rewarded for being faithful to the Lord.

Samuel grew up to become a very important leader and speaker for God. He was a blessing to all the people of Israel because Hannah kept her promise to God about her son.

We can ask God for all kinds of things, but He is most likely to give us the things that help other people. Don't ever be afraid to ask God for good things. Then be sure to use them to make the world a better place.

(Adapted from 1 Samuel 1–2)

"TAKE PITY ON ME, LORD"
A Mother's Prayer for Her Daughter

In Bible times, Tyre and Sidon were cities known for their wickedness. Yet some people from these places wanted to hear from Jesus. They would come in crowds to hear Him preach and teach.

One day, a woman came to ask for Jesus' help. She cried out to Him, "Take pity on me, Lord, Son of David! My daughter has a demon and is very troubled."

To have a demon in Bible times was terrible. The demon somehow controlled the girl's mind and body. Still, this mother loved her daughter dearly. And she believed that Jesus could rescue the girl from the demon.

At first, Jesus did not speak a word to the mother. His friends, the disciples, wondered why. If Jesus wasn't going to help her, they wanted her to leave them alone. So they urged Jesus, "Send her away! She keeps calling us."

Jesus replied, "I was only sent to help the Jewish people who are lost."

Then the mother got down before Jesus. She said, "Lord, help me!" Though she was not Jewish, she believed Jesus was worthy of worship. She believed Jesus alone could help her daughter.

Then Jesus said something strange: "It is not right to take the children's bread and throw it to the dogs." He was not being mean. Jesus was testing the woman to see what her response would be. He wanted to know that her faith in Him was real.

She passed that test with her reply: "Yes, Lord, but even dogs eat the pieces that fall from their owners' tables."

At that clever and faith-filled response, Jesus said to her, "You have much faith. So you will have what you asked for." And her daughter was healed at that very moment. Jesus didn't even have to go see or touch the woman's daughter. He simply spoke the words, and the demon was gone!

Jesus was doing more than testing the mother's faith. He was also teaching everyone who was watching. In that time, Jews often called anyone who was not Jewish a dog. So Jesus was showing that while He came *first* to God's chosen ones, the Jewish people of Israel, He also came for *all* people who choose to believe in Him. It didn't matter then what land or people they were from—and it doesn't matter now. Jesus came to save us all.

(Adapted from Matthew 15; Mark 7)

"SAY THAT MY TWO SONS MAY SIT WITH YOU"

Salome's Prayer for Her Sons

Do you remember that two of Jesus' disciples, the brothers James and John, were called the Sons of Thunder by Jesus? They had been fishermen, just like their father, Zebedee, but they left their boats and nets to become disciples of Jesus when He called them.

The mother of the Sons of Thunder was bold too. Her name was Salome. One day Salome came to Jesus with her sons and got down on her knees before Him to ask something.

So Jesus said to her, "What do you want?"

She replied, "Say that my two sons may sit with You, one at Your right side and one at Your left side, when You are King."

Jesus said to her, "You do not know what you are asking." And to James and John, He asked, "Are you able to take the suffering that I am about to take?"

The Sons of Thunder said, "Yes, we are able."

Jesus said to them, "You will suffer as I will suffer. But the places at My side are not Mine to give. Whoever My Father says will have those places."

Like many good mothers, Salome wanted the very best for her children. Good mothers pray for and encourage their children. They care for them well and provide for them well. They cook their favorite foods and cheer them on in their work and activities. They take great pride in watching them succeed. But good mothers must be careful because sometimes they focus too much on what they think is best for their children rather than what God knows is best.

Salome prayed to Jesus for a big blessing for her children, but Jesus didn't answer her prayer the way she hoped. Yet Salome still remained faithful and close to Jesus. She was one of the women looking on when Jesus died on the cross. How heartbroken she must have been! But she was also one of the first women to discover Jesus was alive again. And how happy she must have been then!

God greatly blesses the mothers who are faithful followers of Jesus, even when He doesn't always answer their prayers for their children the way they want or expect. You can help to be a blessing by being an obedient and respectful child. Children who please their parents please God!

(Adapted from Matthew 20)

JUNE

Prayers of Fathers

In June, the month of Father's Day, we honor and celebrate our dads and those who are like fathers to us. We give them presents and make them treats; we hug them tight and kiss their cheeks! We let them know what a blessing they are to us and tell them all the things we appreciate about them. We should especially appreciate a dad who prays! A loving dad who prays for his children is an extra-special treasure. His prayers are so heartfelt and important. He wants the very best for his children, and he prays to God to ask for His blessings and protection and good gifts for them. He loves to take care of his children, but he knows that sometimes he can't. He also knows that it's ultimately God who takes care of them in all things. We can learn from what God's Word shares with us about Bible-time fathers and their prayers for their children. Read the following stories this month and see for yourself!

"PUT YOUR HAND ON HER THAT SHE MAY BE HEALED"

Jairus' Prayer for His Daughter

Jairus was an important Jewish man, a religious ruler in the synagogue of Capernaum. He was also a father to a beloved daughter. When the girl was twelve years old, she grew very, very sick—maybe with a fiery fever or an awful skin disease. Whatever her illness was, we know that she was much loved by her father and mother and others.

One day when Jesus was near the seashore, surrounded by a crowd of people, Jairus came and got down on his knees before Him. He cried out, saying, "My daughter is almost dead. Please come and put Your hand on her that she may be healed and live." So Jesus went with Jairus.

Everywhere Jesus went, there were miracles. Another one happened on the way to Jairus' house! In the crowd following Jesus was a woman who had been sick for twelve years with bleeding that would not stop. She had gone to many doctors and spent all of her money trying to get better. But she had only gotten worse. Still, she had hope. This woman had heard about Jesus and had come to see Him. And then she simply touched His coat. For she said to herself, "If I can only touch His coat, I will be healed." At the very moment she touched Jesus' coat, her bleeding stopped! She felt in her body that she was healed of her sickness. How powerful Jesus is! No wonder Jairus wanted Jesus to come to his daughter. Jairus believed Jesus could simply put His hand on his daughter and she would live. And Jairus was right.

Jesus told Jairus not to be afraid but to believe, and once he got to Jairus' home, He went to the room where the daughter lay. Jesus told the many people crying for her that she was only sleeping. But it was clear to them that the young girl had died. Then Jesus told everyone except Jairus and his wife to leave the room. He took their daughter by the hand and said, "Little girl, get up!" Right away, she got up, good as new! Do you think she danced and jumped around as she celebrated with her mom and dad?

Even in his high position, Jairus was not full of pride. Instead, he was willing to go to Jesus humbly and ask for help. That's something all of us should do.

(Adapted from Matthew 9; Mark 5; Luke 8)

"LORD, HAVE PITY ON MY SON!"
A Father's Prayer for His Demon-Possessed Boy

One day a father got down on his knees before Jesus. He prayed, "Lord, have pity on my son. Please help him! A demon takes him and won't let him talk. The demon takes hold of him and makes him shake. Spit runs from his mouth, and he grinds his teeth. Wherever the demon takes him, it throws him down. The demon won't leave, and my son is getting weaker."

The poor father's heart broke for his son. He was very troubled because he didn't know what to do. He had asked the disciples to cast out the demon, but they could not. Still, he had hope.

Jesus said, "Bring your son to Me."

So they brought the boy to Jesus. The demon saw Jesus and at once held the boy in its power. The boy fell to the ground with spit running from his mouth. Then Jesus asked, "How long has he been like this?"

The father said, "He's been like this since he was a tiny boy. Many times, the demon throws him into the fire and into the water to kill him. If You can do anything to help us, take pity on us!"

Jesus said to him, "Why do you say *if* I can? The one who has faith can do all things."

At once the father cried out with tears in his eyes, "Lord, I have faith. Help my weak faith to be stronger!"

Jesus spoke sharp words to the demon. He said, "Come out of him! Do not ever go into him again." The demon gave a cry. It threw the boy down and came out of him. The boy was so still and lifeless at first that the people said, "He is dead!" But Jesus took the boy by the hand and helped him up. Then Jesus gave the boy back to his grateful father.

Later the disciples came to Jesus when He was alone. They asked, "Why were we not able to put the demon out?" Jesus said to them, "Because you have so little faith. I tell you, if you only have faith as small as a mustard seed, you could say to this mountain, 'Move from here to over there,' and it would move over. You will be able to do anything."

All we need is a little faith and we can move mountains too!

(Adapted from Matthew 17; Mark 9)

"PLEASE COME TO CAPERNAUM!"
The Royal Official's Prayer for His Dying Son

Jesus' first miracle on earth was in the town of Cana in Galilee. One day as He was traveling, Jesus returned to Cana. While He was there, an official who worked with the king came to Jesus. The royal official had traveled over twenty miles to Cana—all the way from Capernaum—to meet Jesus and ask Him to help the official's son, who was very sick.

When the official came to Jesus, he asked, "Will You please come to Capernaum to heal my son who is dying?"

Jesus replied, "Unless you see special things and powerful works done, you will not believe."

The royal official said, "Sir, please come with me before my son dies."

But Jesus decided not to go with him. He simply said, "Go on your way. Your son will live."

The royal official put his trust in what Jesus said. He could have been angry and bitter that Jesus did not do exactly as he'd asked. He could have begged Jesus to actually come to his house so that Jesus could put His healing hand on the boy. Instead, the official chose to believe that even from miles away, Jesus had all power to heal.

So the royal official left to make his way home again to Capernaum, believing and trusting in Jesus' promise. As he was on his way, his servants met him along the road. "Your son!" they exclaimed. "He is living!"

Relief and gratitude filled the royal official. "When was it?" he asked. "What time did

my son begin to get well?"

They answered, "Yesterday at one o'clock."

The father was amazed, and his faith in Jesus grew, because he knew one o'clock was the exact time Jesus had said to him, "Your son will live."

What a happy reunion for father and son when the royal official got home. Then he and everyone in his house put their trust in Jesus.

(Adapted from John 4)

~~ "LORD, WHAT WILL YOU GIVE ME? ~~ FOR I HAVE NO CHILD"

Abraham's Prayer for an Heir

Abraham was one of God's special people, and he was called a friend of God. As the years were passing and he was growing older and older, he prayed to God to give him a son, for he had none. In those days, it was the custom that the oldest servant of the household would be the heir of any man who had no son. While Abraham respected and trusted his servant Eliezer, he still longed to have a son of his own. Abraham prayed, "Lord, what will You give me? For I have no child. And the one who is to receive what belongs to me is Eliezer. Because You have not given me a child, he is the one who will be given all I have."

Then the word of the Lord came to him, saying, "Your servant Eliezer will not be given what is yours. But a son who will come from you will be given what is yours."

Then God took Abraham outside and said, "Now look up into the heavens and add up the stars, if you are able to count them." God knew it was impossible for any human to do! But God said to Abraham, "Your children and your children's children will be as many as the stars."

Abraham must have been amazed by this. An old man with no children would have as many descendants as the stars in the night sky? He must have thought, *Impossible!* But everything is possible with God. Hard to believe? Yes! Abraham could have laughed at God's words. But he believed in the Lord, and that made him right with God. Abraham

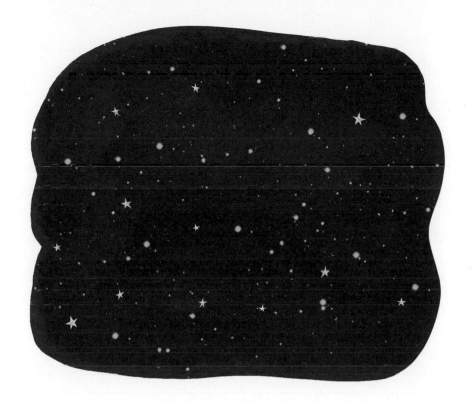

trusted God, and so he was considered righteous.

God's promises are always true, even when He takes His time in making them happen. The promised son, Isaac, was born when Abraham was one hundred years old and Sarah was ninety! Isaac's name means "laughter." His mom, Sarah, had laughed in disbelief when God said she would have a son in her old age. But God had responded, "Is anything too hard for the Lord?"

Abraham, a faithful, praying father, knew the answer to that question was, "Surely not!"

(Adapted from Genesis 15; 18; 21)

Prayers for Forgiveness

In July, people in the United States celebrate the freedom of America with flags and fireworks and family picnics. It's all so much fun! But you can celebrate an even better freedom in your heart all year long. You can have spiritual freedom because Jesus can forgive us from the sins (the bad things we say and think and do) that trap us. You know how good it feels to tell someone you're sorry after you've done something wrong and to hear them say it's okay, so you know forgiveness is a wonderful gift! When we admit our sins to Jesus and tell Him we're sorry and that we need Him to be our Savior, He forgives all our sins forever. That's such a huge relief because we all make mistakes and bad choices sometimes. And because Jesus forgives us so well, we should want to do our best to keep away from sin and forgive others too. The stories in the Bible of times when people prayed to God for forgiveness help us learn why it's so important. Read the following stories this month and see for yourself!

"TAKE AWAY THE SNAKES"
Moses' Prayer for Forgiveness for the Israelites

Do you remember how God's people, the Israelites, were slaves in Egypt? But then God sent plagues—like the bloody river, frogs and flies, skin sores and hail and locusts, and finally death—across the land of Egypt until Pharaoh finally agreed to let God's people go. Then God used Moses to lead His people out of Egypt, and they wandered in the desert for many years. Remember how they grumbled and complained and made God angry, especially when they made a golden calf to worship? But God forgave them when Moses prayed on their behalf.

After many years of wandering in the wilderness and hoping to settle in the promised land, one day they were feeling crabby again. And they were grumbling again. They spoke against God and Moses, saying, "Why have you brought us out of Egypt to die in the desert? There is no food and no water."

God was not pleased with their bad attitudes and complaints. He was very upset with their behavior, and they were in big trouble. So He punished them to teach them a lesson. These were no ordinary consequences—not just going to bed early or doing extra chores or missing out on something fun. No, God sent poisonous snakes! Mean and nasty snakes. The snakes bit the people, and many of the people died. It was a horrible and scary time, and many of the Israelites wished they had never grumbled and complained. They were very sorry for their sins. They came to Moses and said, "We have sinned by speaking against the Lord and you. Please pray to the Lord. Please pray that He will take away the snakes from us."

Then Moses prayed that God would forgive the Israelites and take away the snakes. And God listened and answered Moses with specific instructions. "Make a special snake and put it up on a long wooden pole. Everyone who is bitten will live when they look at it." So Moses made a brass snake and put it at the top of a long piece of wood. If a snake bit anyone, they would live when they looked at the brass snake.

Once again, God showed His great love and mercy for His people even when they sinned against Him. He was willing to forgive them when they humbled themselves and admitted they had done wrong. God's perfect forgiveness freed them from the fear of the snakes and the guilty weight of their sins.

(Adapted from Numbers 21)

~~ "O LORD, HEAR! O LORD, FORGIVE!" ~~
Daniel's Prayer for Forgiveness of Israel's Sins

Do you remember how God rescued Daniel from the lions' den? That same Daniel often had incredible visions and dreams, and he prayed heartfelt prayers. One day he begged God to remember His promise to return the Israelites to their land.

Daniel prayed to God and did not eat. He wore uncomfortable clothes and covered himself with ashes. First he praised God, saying, "Lord, You are great, and we fear You. You keep Your promises and show loving-kindness to those who love You."

Then Daniel confessed the sins of the people. He prayed, "We have done wrong. We have turned against You. We have not listened to Your servants who spoke for You. You are right and good, O Lord. But we are all covered with shame because we have not been faithful to You. But, Lord, You are kind and forgiving, even though we've disobeyed You. We've earned the curses and punishments that You have poured out on us, which were written about in the Law of God's servant Moses. God has done what He said He would do against us and our leaders and has brought much trouble on us. Yet we have not looked for the favor of the Lord our God by turning from our sin and following Your truth."

And then Daniel asked God for His forgiveness and goodness and blessing, saying, "O Lord, because You are right and good in what You do, do not be angry any longer with Your city Jerusalem. For because of our sins and the sins of our fathers, Jerusalem and Your people have been put to shame by everyone around us. So now, our God, please listen to my prayer. Look with favor on the house of God that now lies in waste. Please, God, open Your eyes and see our trouble. We are not asking this of You because we are right or good but because of Your great loving-pity. O Lord, hear! O Lord, forgive! O Lord, listen and act! For Your glory, God, do not wait. Because Your city and Your people are called by Your name."

Daniel's prayer shows us what it means to be faithful to God. He taught us how to pray with praise and confession and humble requests to receive God's forgiveness.

(Adapted from Daniel 9)

"FATHER, FORGIVE THEM!"
Jesus' Prayer for the People Crucifying Him

Near the end of Jesus' life on earth, He predicted what would happen before He died. And all those things started to come true. His friend Judas helped soldiers find and capture Jesus in exchange for thirty pieces of silver. Then those soldiers took Jesus to the Jewish leaders who hated Him. They accused Jesus of bad things He'd never done! From there, Jesus was taken to the palace of Pilate, the Roman governor. Pilate did not believe in Jesus, but he didn't want to kill Him either. "I find nothing wrong in this Man," Pilate said. But he handed Jesus over to His enemies. They spit on Jesus and put a painful crown of sharp thorns on His head. They mocked Him and taunted Him and beat Him up.

Pilate tried again to free Jesus. He called together the people who wanted to kill Jesus and said, "You brought this Man to me as one who leads the people in the wrong way, but I do not find Him guilty of the things you say. King Herod found nothing wrong with Him either, because he sent Him back to us. There is no reason to have Him put to death. I will punish Him and let Him go free."

But the Jewish people who hated Jesus insisted that He should die. They even demanded that Barabbas, a man who had killed people and caused all kinds of trouble, go free instead of Jesus. They yelled out, "Nail Jesus to a cross!" Over and over they shouted, "Crucify Him! Crucify Him!"

So Pilate said to them a third time, "Why? What bad thing has He done? I have found no reason to put Him to death."

But they kept shouting and yelling that He must be killed. And finally, Pilate gave in. He let Barabbas go free and he gave Jesus over to the angry crowd.

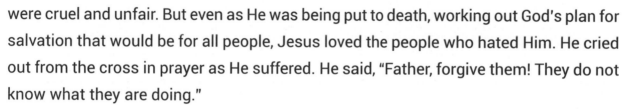

Jesus had done nothing wrong, but the people who hated Him were cruel and unfair. But even as He was being put to death, working out God's plan for salvation that would be for all people, Jesus loved the people who hated Him. He cried out from the cross in prayer as He suffered. He said, "Father, forgive them! They do not know what they are doing."

No one else has ever had such amazing love and forgiveness for people as Jesus Christ. He suffered and died to take away sin and free all who trust in Him as Savior.

(Adapted from Luke 22–23; John 19)

"LORD, DO NOT HOLD THIS SIN AGAINST THEM"

Stephen's Prayer for His Killers

After Jesus died on the cross, He rose again and went up to heaven. Then God's Holy Spirit came to live inside Jesus' followers. As more and more people became believers, Jesus' church grew. Church leaders chose helpers to care for people in need. Stephen was chosen to help give out food.

Stephen was a Christian who was full of faith and power. He spoke with the wisdom of the Holy Spirit. But some of the religious leaders who had hated Jesus hated Stephen too. "We have heard him say things against Moses and God," they said. In this way they got the people talking against Stephen. They took him to the religious leaders' court where people lied about him. But even though people were trying to get him in trouble, Stephen was strong and calm and full of peace. His face even looked like the face of an angel!

The head religious leader asked Stephen, "Are these things true?"

Stephen didn't even try to defend himself. He was mostly concerned about saying what God wanted him to share. So he preached a message about the history of Israel and the nation's relationship with God. Stephen boldly told the religious leaders they were wrong to reject and kill Jesus. The final words of his message were, "You have hard hearts and ears that will not listen to me! You are always working against the Holy Spirit. Your early fathers did too. They killed those who told of the coming of Jesus. Now you have handed Him over and killed Him. You had the Law given to you by angels. Yet you have not kept it."

When Stephen finished speaking, the religious leaders in the court were furious. But Stephen was filled with the Holy Spirit. As he looked up to heaven, he saw the shining-greatness of God and Jesus. He said, "I see

heaven open and the Son of Man standing at the right side of God!"

The religious leaders grew even angrier. They grabbed Stephen, dragged him out of the city, and began to throw stones at him to kill him.

Stephen knew he would soon die. But even as he suffered, he fell on his knees and prayed for the people killing him. Stephen cried out in a loud voice, "Lord, do not hold this sin against them."

True forgiveness means we don't hold sin against anyone. We set them free from our desire to pay them back—no matter how awfully they behaved. Since we've been forgiven by Jesus, we can offer forgiveness to others like Stephen did.

(Adapted from Acts 6–7)

AUGUST

Prayers for Victory in Battle

Imagine that you have to take a long walk on the hottest summer day in August. The sun beats down with no mercy, and there's not even a breeze to cool you a little. You just took your last sip of water, and you still have a mile to go. Ugh! It sure takes perseverance to make it through the worst days of summer. And it sure takes perseverance to make it through all kinds of other challenges too. We need God's help! We need Him to give us victory over the tough times and people and situations that come against us. In the Bible, we learn about people who prayed for God to give them victory over the tough battles they found themselves in. They can encourage and inspire us when we need victory over our battles too. Read the following stories this month and see for yourself!

"SUN AND MOON, STAND STILL!"
Joshua's Prayer for a Miracle

Joshua was a faithful and courageous man who became the leader of the people of Israel after Moses died.

One day, Joshua found himself facing several enemies who had teamed up together. The king of Jerusalem heard that Joshua had destroyed a city called Ai. He also heard that the people of Gibeon had made peace with Israel and were living among them. That made him very afraid—because Gibeon was a large city, and all its men were strong. So the king of Jerusalem sent word to four other kings. He said to them, "Come and help me. Let's go fight against Gibeon. For it has made peace with Joshua and the people of Israel." So the five kings gathered together with all their armies. And they went and set up their tents by Gibeon, ready to fight.

Then the men of Gibeon sent word to Joshua. "Don't leave us alone! Hurry and help us!" they said. "For all the kings who live in the hill country have gathered against us."

So Joshua gathered all his warriors and strong soldiers. The Lord said to Joshua, "Don't be afraid of them. For I have already helped you win this battle.

So Joshua snuck up on them by surprise after traveling all night. The Lord brought trouble and destruction on the kings and their armies in front of Israel, and they ran away! And while they ran, the Lord made large hailstones fall from heaven on them.

Then Joshua spoke to the Lord on that day and said, "Sun and moon, stand still!" He was asking God to stop the sun and moon—and God did it. The sun stood still and the moon stopped until the nation of Israel punished those who fought against them. That's

right—the sun stopped in the center of the sky! It did not hurry to go down for nearly a whole day. There had been no day like it ever before, and there has been no day like it since. The Lord listened to Joshua, and the Lord fought for Israel. Then Joshua and the Israelite army returned to their tents.

The Lord fought for Israel and helped them win. Then He showed His power as the one true God over all creation—all powerful even over the sun and moon! The Lord fights for us to help us win life's battles too. Just ask for His help.

(Adapted from Joshua 10)

~ "GIVE ME STRENGTH ONCE MORE!" ~
Samson's Prayer to Defeat the Philistines

God gave Samson's mother and father special rules for his life even before the boy was born. An angel of the Lord told Samson's mom, "You will soon give birth to a son. His hair must never be cut. He will be dedicated to God from birth. He will begin to rescue Israel from the Philistines." She named the baby Samson, and God blessed him as he grew up.

God gave Samson incredible strength. One day as he was traveling, a lion attacked Samson. But the Spirit of the Lord powerfully filled Samson. He ripped the lion's jaws apart with his bare hands as if the lion were a baby goat!

Throughout his life, Samson fought with the Philistines. And the Philistines wondered how one man could have such incredible strength. One day some Philistine rulers came to Samson's girlfriend, Delilah. They promised to give her lots of money if she could trick Samson into sharing the secret of his great strength so they could know how to beat him. Delilah agreed to the plan.

At first, Samson would only tease Delilah when she asked him to share the truth about his strength. But after she begged and nagged Samson for days, he finally told her, "My hair has never been cut because I have been set apart for God since the day I was born. If my head were shaved, my strength would leave me." Delilah then lulled Samson to sleep on her lap and called a man in to cut off all Samson's hair.

When Samson woke up, at first he did not realize that the Lord had left him because his hair was cut. He tried to fight, but the Philistines captured him. They cut out his eyes and put him in prison.

Later on, the leaders of the Philistines gathered to make fun of Samson. They made him stand between the stone pillars that held up the temple they were in.

Samson's hair had grown again while he was in prison. Now he called out to God and said, "O Lord God, please remember me. Give me strength once more so that I can punish the Philistines." Then Samson took hold of the two pillars that held up the building. He pushed against them with all his strength so that the temple building fell. The Philistine leaders and thousands of Philistine people were killed. Samson died along with them, but God had worked out His plans through Samson—strong and powerful plans to free the Israelite people from the rule of the evil Philistines.

We too can pray to God for special strength. It might not be the power to knock down a building, but God will give us strength to get through all kinds of hard things. He will lead us to victory to bring about His good plans.

(Adapted from Judges 13–16)

"ANSWER ME SO THESE PEOPLE MAY KNOW THAT YOU ARE GOD!"

Elijah's Prayer for Fire from Heaven

Elijah was a faithful prophet of God. One day during a great drought and famine, God said to Elijah, "Go speak to the evil king Ahab, and I will send rain down on the earth." So Elijah went to Ahab.

When King Ahab saw Elijah, he said, "Is it you, the one who brings trouble to Israel?"

Elijah replied, "I have not brought trouble to Israel. But you have because you turned away from the Lord and followed the false god Baal. So now, call together people from all over Israel to meet me at Mount Carmel. And gather together 450 men who speak for Baal."

Ahab did as Elijah said. Then Elijah came near all the people and said, "If the Lord is God, follow Him. But if Baal is god, then follow him." The people did not respond.

Then Elijah said to them, "I am the only man left who speaks for God. But here are 450 men who speak for Baal. Bring us some wood. Then you call on the name of your god, and I will call on the name of the Lord. The God who answers by creating fire is the one true God." All the people thought this battle of gods was a good idea.

So Elijah said to the men who spoke for Baal, "Call on the name of your god." They called on the name of Baal from morning until noon, saying, "O Baal, answer us." But no one answered. They jumped and danced around the altar they had made. Still, no one answered.

At noon Elijah made fun of them. He said, "Call out with a loud voice. Maybe he's

asleep." So they cried with a loud voice until evening. But no one answered. No one listened.

Then Elijah said to all the people, "Come near to me." So they did. Elijah built an altar in the name of the Lord, and he made a large ditch around it. Then he set the wood in place. He said, "Fill four jars with water and pour it on the wood." Then he said, "Do it a second time." And then, "Do it a third time." The water filled the ditch.

Elijah prayed, "O Lord, I am Your servant and have done all these things at Your word. Answer me so these people may know that You are God. Turn their hearts to You."

The fire of the Lord fell. Even though everything on and around the altar was soaking wet, the fire burned up the wood, the stones, and the dust. It even picked up the water in the ditch! All the people fell on their faces in awe. They said, "The Lord, He is God!"

Then God, who always wins over false gods, sent rain on the land.

(Adapted from 1 Kings 18)

"LORD, THERE IS NO ONE BUT YOU TO HELP IN THE BATTLE!"
Asa's Prayer for Victory

King Asa was a good king of Judah who did what was right in the eyes of the Lord. He tore down the pillars and altars that had been used to worship false gods before his reign began. He told Judah to follow the one true God and obey His laws. And the nation had peace under his rule—no one fought a war with Judah, and King Asa built strong cities during those years of peace. So he said to the people of Judah, "The land is still ours because we have followed the Lord our God. We have followed Him, and He has given us rest on every side." So they kept doing well because they followed the one true God.

But then their time of peace ended. A king named Zerah came out to fight against them. And he came out with a huge army, an army much bigger than the army of Judah.

King Asa had a lot of soldiers, brave men with shields and spears and bows and arrows. But they couldn't compare with Zerah's huge army of a million men and 300 war wagons! Still, Asa bravely went out to meet him. Both armies made themselves ready for battle.

Asa knew there was no way the smaller and weaker army of Judah could defeat Zerah's big army without help from God. So Asa called to the Lord God and prayed, "Lord, there is no one but You to help in the battle between the powerful and the weak. So help us, please! For we trust in You. In Your name we have come against these many people. O Lord, You are our God. Do not let any army win the fight against You."

And God answered Asa's prayer. God began to destroy Judah's enemies right before the eyes of Asa and his people. The enemy ran away! Asa and the people with him went after them. Judah's enemies were destroyed. The people of Judah destroyed all the nearby cities and took every valuable thing that was in them. Then they returned to Jerusalem.

When he was in trouble, Asa prayed to God. The king knew that even though the enemy was more powerful, God could still help Judah win the battle. With God as our leader, we always walk away victorious.

(Adapted from 2 Chronicles 14)

SEPTEMBER

Silly Prayers

Back-to-school time is either exciting or scary or sad—or maybe a little of all three. There are a lot of feelings when the fun of summer break ends and a new year of school begins. But we should be so thankful to God for the amazing brains He has given us. It's incredible how we can learn new things every single day. So in the times you might feel bored and blah about school, choose to thank God instead. Thank Him that He gave you such a powerful mind. Use it to learn about God and worship Him, and then ask Him to show you all the good things He designed you to know and do. The Bible tells us about some people who did not use their brains very well when they prayed—you don't want to act like them. They should have been a lot smarter in their prayers, and we can learn from their mistakes. Read the following stories this month and see for yourself!

"O LORD GOD, FOR SURE YOU HAVE FOOLED THESE PEOPLE!"

Jeremiah's Prayer Accusing God

Jeremiah was a prophet of God. God chose Jeremiah before he was even born. The Lord said, "Before I even formed you in your mother's womb, I knew you. Before you were born, I decided you were holy. I chose you to speak to the nations for Me."

Jeremiah replied, "God, I don't know how to speak! I am only a boy."

But God said, "Do not say, 'I am only a boy.' Go everywhere I send you, and say whatever I tell you. Don't be afraid. For I am with you to help you get out of trouble."

Then God put out His hand and touched Jeremiah's mouth and said to him, "See, I have put My words in your mouth. I have chosen you today to be over the nations and the kings, to destroy and throw down, to build and plant."

God told Jeremiah that he should not marry or have children. The Lord wanted Jeremiah to devote himself fully to speaking for God.

Jeremiah was sometimes called the weeping prophet. He was sad and cried a lot over the wicked ways of the people of Israel—because he knew God would punish them.

And though Jeremiah walked closely with God, he was not perfect. He got depressed at times. One time he prayed in a very silly way. He forgot God's goodness and truth and faithfulness, and he allowed himself to be discouraged and doubtful of God. He even began to accuse God of being dishonest with the people of Israel. He prayed, "O Lord God, for sure You have fooled these people! You told them, 'You will have peace,' when in truth,

a sword brings danger to their lives."

But God never lies. The Bible says He *cannot* lie. And so Jeremiah needed to learn a lesson from his silly prayer. He needed to trust again that God was working out His good plans, even if Jeremiah did not fully understand them. So that's what he did. No matter the sadness and pain that sometimes came from obeying God in this world, Jeremiah kept trusting God. He believed that God was teaching and loving and disciplining His people—and always providing a way for them to repent of their sin and be saved.

(Adapted from Jeremiah 1–4)

"NO, I COULD NEVER DO THAT, GOD!"
Ezekiel's Prayer of Protest

Ezekiel was a prophet whose name means "strengthened by God." He preached to the people of his day about God's judgment and salvation. Sometimes God told Ezekiel to do some strange things to warn people about the danger of their sin. One day God said to Ezekiel, "Get a hard block of clay. Set it down in front of you, and draw the city of Jerusalem on it. Then build a wall around the city of clay to shut it in. You will fight a battle against it. This will be something special for the people of Israel to see."

Next God told Ezekiel to lie on his left side for 390 days. This was a sign to the nation of Israel that they would be punished for 390 years because they had turned away from God. God said, "Lie on your left side, and I will lay the people's sin on you. You will be under the weight of their sin for all the days you lie on your side."

God wanted to show people that there are consequences for sin. However, God is never happy when people are punished for their sins. He wants people to turn away from sin so He can give them the best kind of life. They can only have this kind of life through faith and obedience to Him. God said to Ezekiel, "Tell the people of Israel that I am not pleased when sinful people die. But I am pleased when they turn from their sin and live. Turn! Turn from your sinful ways, O people of Israel!"

Ezekiel must have wondered why God chose such odd ways to share His warnings and prophecies. And one day Ezekiel prayed in a silly way to God. When God told him to eat food that Ezekiel thought was unclean, the prophet said, "No, I could never do that, God!" But even as Ezekiel questioned God, the Lord loved him. And God kept using Ezekiel to speak to His beloved people of Israel.

God might work in ways that seem strange, but He is always working in ways that are best. And God's ways always lead to His perfect endings.

(Adapted from Ezekiel 2; 4; 22; 33)

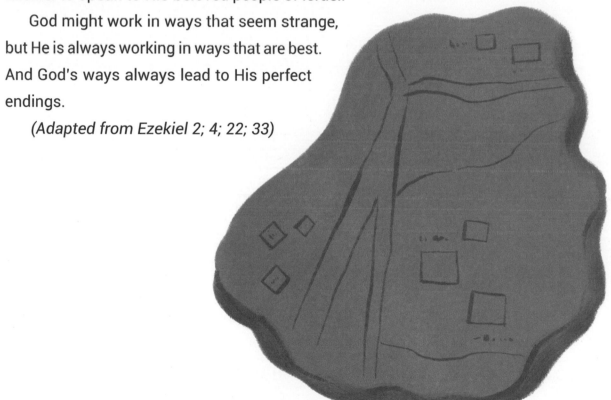

"O LORD, WHY HAVE YOU HURT THESE PEOPLE?"

Moses' Prayer of Complaint to God

Before all those plagues God sent on Egypt, before the people of Israel were finally set free from their slavery, Moses had a lot of hard work to do. He had to tell the strong, scary Pharaoh that he was doing wrong! Sometimes Moses didn't think he could do what God asked. When God first called him to go to Pharaoh and lead God's people out of Egypt, Moses said, "Lord, I am not a man of words. I have never been. For I talk slowly, and it is difficult for me to speak."

So God said to him, "Who makes someone not able to speak or hear? Who makes someone blind or able to see? Is it not I, the Lord? So go now. And I will be with your mouth. I will teach you what to say."

But Moses still argued. He said, "O Lord, please, I beg you, send some other person—not me!"

This made God angry, but still he loved Moses. God even listened to Moses' silly prayer. "Aaron is your brother, and I know he can speak well," God said. "He is coming to meet you. You must speak to him and put the words in his mouth. I will be with your mouth and his mouth. I will teach you what you are to do. He will speak to the people for you. You will take this special stick in your hand and use it to make special things happen for the people to see."

But even with Aaron's help, it was no easy job to warn Pharaoh. He didn't want to let God's people go because they were slaves doing lots of free work for him. Pharaoh said, "Why should I obey your God and let Israel go? I do not know the Lord. And I will not let Israel go." Then he made the Israelites work even harder. He said, "Let more work be given to the men so they will not have time to listen to Moses' lies." Pharaoh punished the people when they couldn't do the impossible things he commanded.

The Israelites complained to Moses and Aaron, and Moses grew very discouraged. He prayed to God, "O Lord, why have You hurt these people? Why did you ever send me? Since I went to Pharaoh to speak in Your name, he has only hurt these people more. You have not set Your people free at all."

But Moses was forgetting that God works things out in His own ways, in His own perfect timing. God had not set the people free—yet—but He would. God always keeps His promises. And He told Moses, "Now you will see what I will do to Pharaoh. For he will be made to let them go because of My strong hand."

(Adapted from Exodus 4–6)

~~ "GOD, I THANK YOU THAT I AM ~~ NOT LIKE OTHER MEN"

The Pharisee's Prideful Prayer

When Jesus lived on earth and taught people about God, He often used picture stories called parables. One day, His followers asked Him, "Why do You teach in picture stories?"

He answered them, "This is why I speak in picture stories. The people have eyes, but they do not see. They have ears, but they do not hear or understand. This is exactly what the prophet Isaiah said would happen." Jesus wants everyone to have eyes and ears and hearts that pay attention and understand God's truth.

One of Jesus' picture stories was about a silly way to pray and a good way to pray. He told this story to some people who were full of pride. These people did not think well of others; they mostly bragged and thought only about themselves. So Jesus said, "Two men went up to the house of God to pray. One of them was a Pharisee, a proud religious law keeper. The other was a man who collected taxes. The proud Pharisee stood and prayed like this: 'God, I thank You that I am not like other men. I am not like those who steal. I am not like those who sin. I am not even like this tax collector. I go without food two times a week so I can pray better. I always give away part of the money I earn.'"

Jesus continued, "But the tax collector stood a long way off. He would not even lift his eyes to heaven. He hit himself on his chest and said, 'God, have pity on me! I am a sinner!'" Then Jesus explained, "I tell you, this man went back to his house forgiven, and not the other man. For whoever makes himself look more important than he is will find out how little he is worth. Whoever does not try to brag about himself will be made important."

Telling God how wonderful you are, without admitting your sins and mistakes, is a silly way to pray. It is better to tell God how wonderful and good *He* is. Then be humble and honest about your own sins and mistakes. We can be grateful that God loves and forgives us no matter what.

(Adapted from Matthew 13; Luke 18)

OCTOBER

Prayers for Wisdom

The harvest season is a time to be thankful for the good things that were grown all summer long—apples and pumpkins and other yummy fruits and vegetables. Does your mouth water when you think of your favorite fall foods? We can be grateful for the farmers who help us have such wonderful treats! If those farmers don't work hard at sowing (which means planting seeds) and then tending the crops with care, they will never get to celebrate the reaping, which is all about gathering up the goodness. While farmers sow seeds to grow plants, we can sow in prayer. We sow in prayer by talking with God and taking good care of our relationship with Him. We ask Him for what we need, and we ask Him to protect and bless and teach and guide us. When we pray like that, we reap wisdom and closeness with our heavenly Father. That sure is a gathering of goodness! The Bible tells us about people who sowed in prayer and reaped in wisdom from God, and we can learn from their examples. Read the following stories this month and see for yourself!

"LORD, YOU KNOW THE HEARTS OF ALL MEN"

The Disciples' Prayer for Wisdom in Replacing Judas

After Jesus had suffered and died on the cross, He rose again! After His resurrection, He proved Himself alive by showing Himself to many people for forty days and teaching about the kingdom of God.

One day with His disciples, Jesus said, "You will receive power when the Holy Spirit comes into your lives. You will tell about Me in the city of Jerusalem and over all the countries and to the ends of the earth." Then, while they were looking at Him, He was taken up to heaven! A cloud carried Him away so they could not see Him. They were still looking up to heaven, watching Him go, when two men dressed in white suddenly stood beside them. They said, "Why are you still standing here looking up to heaven? Jesus will return in the same way you saw Him go up."

So Jesus' followers decided to go back to Jerusalem. When they came into the city, they went up to a room on the second floor where they stayed and prayed together. Women who followed Jesus—including Mary, His mother—were there, along with Jesus' brothers.

Not long after, Peter realized it was time to replace the disciple Judas, who had turned against Jesus. He got up in front of about 120 followers of Jesus and said, "It happened as the Scriptures said it would. They told about Judas, who would betray Jesus and hand Him over to be killed. Judas was one of our group and had a part in our work. But he is gone now." Peter went on, "The man to take the place of Judas should be one of these men who walked along with us when the Lord Jesus was on earth. He must have been with us from the day Jesus was baptized by John to the day Jesus was taken up to heaven so he can tell others that he saw Jesus raised from the dead."

JOSEPH

MATTHIAS

So they brought two men in front of the big group of followers. Their names were Joseph and Matthias. Then the followers prayed together, "Lord, You know the hearts of all men. Show us which of these two men You have chosen to take the place of Judas and be a missionary." Then they drew names, and the name of Matthias was chosen. He was added to the group of disciples.

God knows the hearts of all people. Like Jesus' followers back in Bible times, let's pray together with other believers for His wisdom, His leading, and His will to be done.

(Adapted from Acts 1)

"GIVE ME AN UNDERSTANDING HEART"
Solomon's Prayer for Wisdom

King David of Israel had said to his son Solomon, "Be strong and do what the Lord your God tells you. Walk in His ways. Keep His laws and His Word. Then you will succeed in all that you do and in every place you go." And when David died, Solomon became the new king of Israel.

King Solomon wanted to do as his father, David, had said. He wanted to follow God's ways and keep God's laws, so God wanted to bless Solomon. One night God came to Solomon in a special dream and said, "Ask what you wish Me to give you."

Solomon could have asked God for anything at all, but he said, "God, You have made me king in place of my father, David. But I am only a little child. I do not know how to start or finish. I am among so many of Your people—too many to count! So please give me an understanding heart to judge Your people and know the difference between good and bad."

Solomon had made a very good request! He knew that wisdom from God was far more valuable than any treasure.

Because Solomon had chosen so well, God wanted to bless him even more. He said to Solomon, "You have asked for this and not for a long life for yourself. You have not asked for riches. But you have asked for understanding to know what is right. Because you have asked this, I have done what you said. See, I have given you a wise and understanding heart. No one has been like you before, and no one will ever be like you. And I also give

you what you have not asked. I give you both riches and honor. And if you walk in My ways and keep My laws and Word as your father did, I will allow you to live a long time."

When we choose to ask God for wisdom rather than riches, we also please Him, just like Solomon did. God is our good, heavenly Father who loves to bless us for choosing what's best.

When Solomon woke up from his dream, he returned to Jerusalem. He praised and worshipped God and hosted a great feast for all of his servants. King Solomon did not rule Israel perfectly, but he did many good things. For many years he listened to and learned from God, using the understanding he had asked for. And the people he ruled were amazed because they could see his wisdom from God.

(Adapted from 1 Kings 2–3)

"SHOW ME SOMETHING TO PROVE THAT IT IS YOU WHO SPEAKS WITH ME"

Gideon's Prayer for God's Assurance and Direction

When God's people were under the control of the cruel Midianites, they became very poor and weak. So they cried out to God for help. God sent an angel to remind the people of Israel that even though He had done so much for them in the past, they had disobeyed Him and worshipped fake gods.

Then the angel of the Lord went to an Israelite named Gideon. The man was working to hide his food from the Midianites.

The angel said, "The Lord is with you! You are a mighty hero, a powerful soldier!"

Gideon replied, "Then why has all this happened to us? The Lord has left us alone and put us under the power of the Midianites."

And the angel, who was really God, said, "You are strong, and you can rescue Israel from the Midianites. I am sending you."

Gideon said to Him, "O Lord, how can I save Israel? My family is the weakest around here. And I am the youngest in my father's house."

But God said to him, "For sure I will be with you. You will destroy Midian."

Gideon still wasn't sure. So he asked God, "If I have found favor in Your eyes, please show me something to prove that it is You who speaks with me. I ask of You, do not leave here until I return to You with my gift and lay it before You."

And God said, "I will stay until you return."

Then Gideon went into his house. He prepared some meat and made bread. He put the meat in a basket and the water from boiling the meat in a pot. Then he brought all these things out and set them down in front of a tree.

The angel of God said to him, "Take the meat and the bread and lay them on this rock. Then pour out the water." And Gideon did. Then the angel of the Lord sent fire to burn up the meat and the bread, and the angel disappeared. So Gideon knew that he had seen the angel of the Lord. And he said, "I am afraid, O Lord God! For now I have seen the angel of the Lord face-to-face."

But God said to Gideon, "Peace be with you. Do not be afraid. You will not die."

Then Gideon built an altar there to the Lord. He gave it the name The Lord Is Peace.

It took some time for Gideon to really trust God. But by talking with God and asking for faith, Gideon was able to do amazing things. We can do the same! Talk to God when you're confused or afraid. He'll be happy to give you the wisdom and courage you need.

(Adapted from Judges 6)

"MAY THE LORD CHOOSE SOMEONE WHO WILL LEAD THEM"

Moses' Prayer for a New Leader of Israel

Moses was an extra-special leader and prophet of God. The Lord met him face-to-face. There was no one like him to speak for God in Israel and do such powerful works from God in Egypt. Yet after all Moses did, after leading the Israelites round and round in the wilderness, he was not allowed to enter the land God had promised. How sad!

But why? Because God once told Moses to speak to a rock so that it would pour out much-needed water for the people of Israel. They had been suffering with no water and were very thirsty. But Moses decided to do things his own way rather than God's way. Moses hit the rock with his walking stick! And there were consequences for that big mistake. God said to Moses, "Because you were not faithful to Me that time and you did not honor Me as holy among the people of Israel, you will not go into the land I am giving the people of Israel. You will only see it from far away."

Moses was disappointed, but he still remained faithful to God. When it was nearly time for the people to enter the promised land, Moses knew the people would need a new leader to go with them since he couldn't. He prayed, "May the Lord choose someone who will lead them. Someone to come before this community. That way, the Lord's people will not be like sheep without a shepherd."

Moses could have been bitter and angry because of God's decision not to allow him to enter the promised land. But he wasn't. He loved and honored God. He had wisdom and humility, and he loved the people of Israel and wanted them to have a caring leader. That man turned out to be Joshua.

After Moses prayed, God said, "Take Joshua, son of Nun, a man who has a spirit of leadership, and lay your hand on him. Have him stand before the priest and everyone else, and commission him in their presence. Give him some of your authority so the whole Israelite community will listen to him. Then he and all the Israelites will go out, and at his command, they will come into the land."

Moses obeyed. He took Joshua and laid his hands on him to make him the new leader. Maybe someday *you'll* be a leader among God's people. Right now, learn His Word and obey what it says. That's the best way to prepare for His service.

(*Adapted from Numbers 20; 27; Deuteronomy 34*)

NOVEMBER

Helpless Prayers

Thanksgiving is a time to be grateful for all the good things in your life—your family and your friends, your pets and your home, your toys and all the fun things you get to do. And don't forget the good food you get to eat! You can be thankful for the not-so-good things, too, for the way they help you depend on God's love and care to get you through. Hard times in our lives make us cry out to God in what might feel like hopeless prayers. We feel helpless and can't think of any good answer for the problems we face. But then when we see God answer our prayers in amazing, miraculous ways, we are filled with gratitude like never before! Have you ever been through something like that? The Bible tells us about people who have been, and we can learn from them. Read the following stories this month and see for yourself!

"YOU HAVE BROUGHT ME UP FROM THE PIT, GOD!"

Jonah's Prayer from Inside the Big Fish

Jonah was a man who found himself in the belly of a big fish! How did that happen? Well, the problem started when God said to him, "Go to the city of Nineveh. The people there are very wicked. Tell them I have seen their terrible sins, and I am sending My judgment." But Jonah didn't want to go to Nineveh. He'd heard about how bad it was there, and he

wanted nothing to do with that city or its people. So Jonah tried to run away from God. He got on a boat and set sail for another land.

But God is everywhere, and no matter how he tried, Jonah couldn't run away or hide from Him. God caused a strong wind and a big storm on the sea where Jonah was sailing. The storm was so dangerous that Jonah's boat was about to break up and sink. All the sailors were scared, and they decided that the storm was Jonah's fault. "You'd better throw me into the sea," he said. "Then the seas will calm down. I know this bad storm has happened because of me."

So the sailors prayed to God for mercy and then threw Jonah into the sea. Suddenly, the storm stopped, just like Jonah said it would. Then the sailors worshipped the one true God and promised to serve Him.

God still had plans for Jonah! He sent a big fish to swallow Jonah, but it didn't hurt him. Jonah simply sat in the slimy, stinky stomach of that fish for three days and three nights. While he sat, he prayed. "God, You threw me into the deep waters, to the bottom of the sea. The sea was all around me. Weeds were around my head. I sank down. But You have brought me up from the pit, God! While I was losing all my strength, I remembered You. And my prayer came to You. I will give You what I have promised because You are the one who saves."

Jonah didn't just pray when he felt helpless. He also honored and worshipped God—even from the stomach of a big fish! So we know that no matter how strange or hard or sad something is, we can worship and feel grateful too. And God listens and answers and blesses us when we do.

(Adapted from Jonah 1–2)

"WE ONLY HAVE FIVE LOAVES OF BREAD AND TWO FISH!"

The Disciples' Prayer for Jesus to Help Feed the People

Everywhere Jesus went when He lived on earth, crowds of people wanted to hear Him teach. They came from many different towns as quickly as they could to wherever they learned He was going. One day after Jesus had taken some quiet time, He got off a boat to discover even more people wanting His teaching and His healing. And He felt sorry for them. But it was getting later, and evening was coming. So Jesus' disciples asked Him to send the crowds away. "We're out here in the middle of nowhere," they said. "These people need to go into the towns and buy themselves some food."

But Jesus said, "They don't need to go away. You can give them something to eat."

What? The disciples were confused. They didn't have a market nearby or a kitchen to use. Didn't Jesus see how many people there were? There were a *lot* of them—about five thousand men plus women and children too! "We only have five loaves of bread and two fish, which a young boy gave us," they said to Jesus. They didn't know how to feed so many people with such a small amount of food! They felt totally helpless.

So Jesus said to the disciples, "Bring the loaves of bread and the fish to Me." And they did. Then Jesus told the crowds of people to sit down on the grass. They sat down in big groups, some groups with fifty people and some with one hundred. Jesus took the five loaves of bread and two fish, and He looked up to heaven and gave thanks for them. Then He broke the loaves in pieces and gave them to His disciples, and the disciples

gave them to the people. Jesus cut up the fish, and they shared that with everyone too. Then the five thousand men plus women and children ate and ate some more.

When they were all happy and full, there was still plenty of food left over. The disciples picked up twelve baskets full of extra bread and fish—one basket for each disciple. It was hard to believe all of that came from just five loaves of bread and two fish. What a miracle! Jesus had gone far above and beyond to bless the people with the food they needed. Though the disciples had felt helpless, they learned that when Jesus asks us to do something, even if it seems totally impossible, we can pray to Him. Then He will provide exactly what we need, exactly when we need it!

(Adapted from Matthew 14; Mark 6; Luke 9; John 6)

"THE BURDEN IS TOO MUCH"
Moses' Prayer for Relief

One day when God's people were still wandering in the wilderness, they began to complain about the food that God provided. They had a miracle bread called manna that fell from the sky each night, but they wanted something else. The people whined and cried out, "If only we had meat to eat! We remember the fish we ate in Egypt—also the cucumbers, melons, leeks, onions, and garlic. But now we don't even want to eat because we never see anything but this manna!"

The manna was plain and tasted like something made with olive oil. But it was what God had provided.

God became angry at all the complaining, and Moses was troubled. He questioned the Lord, saying, "Why have You brought this trouble on me, Your servant? What have I done to displease You that You put the burden of all these people on me? Why did You tell me to lead them to the land You promised to their ancestors? Where can I get meat for all these people? They keep wailing to me, 'Give us meat to eat!' I cannot carry all these people by myself! The burden is too much, too heavy for me."

God listened to Moses' cries and said, "Bring Me seventy of Israel's elders who are known as leaders among the people. Have them come to the tent of meeting, that they may stand there with you. I will come down and speak with you there, and I will take some of the power of the Spirit that is on you and put it on them. They will share the burden of the people with you so that you will not have to carry it alone."

God also promised to send meat to the people. "How is that possible?" Moses asked.

The Lord answered, "Is My power limited? Now you will see whether or not what I say will come true for you." God soon sent birds called quail. There were so many that they surrounded the Israelites' camp, and the people gathered up many of them to eat. There was plenty of meat now! But some of the people got sick because of their complaints and ungratefulness.

Moses learned that when he couldn't do a big job, God would listen to his prayers and provide help.

(Adapted from Numbers 11)

"MY GOD, WHY HAVE YOU LEFT ME ALONE?"

Jesus' Prayer on the Cross

When Jesus was about to be crucified, the soldiers and the people who hated Him treated Him terribly. They took off His clothes and put a purple coat on Him. They put a crown of thorns on His head. They put a stick in His right hand and got on their knees before Him to make fun of Him. They mocked Him as they said, "Hello, King of the Jews!" They spit on Him. They hit Him on the head. And after they had made fun of Him, they led Him away to be nailed to a cross.

On the cross, over His head, they put a sign that said, THIS IS JESUS, THE KING OF THE JEWS.

Two robbers were nailed to crosses beside Jesus. One was on His right side, and one was on His left. Those who walked by shook their heads and laughed at Him. They said, "Save Yourself. If You are the Son of God, come down from the cross."

The head religious leaders and the teachers of the Law and the other leaders made fun of Him too. They said, "He saved others, but He cannot save Himself. If He is the King of the Jews, let Him come down from the cross. Then we will believe in Him. Let God save Him now if God cares for Him. Jesus said He was the Son of God."

From noon until three o'clock on that day, it was dark over all the land. At about three o'clock Jesus cried with a loud voice, "My God, My God, why have You left Me alone?" Jesus gave another loud cry and then gave up His spirit and died.

THIS IS JESUS
THE KING OF THE JEWS

Jesus must have felt helpless and alone as He took all the sins of every person, suffering and dying in their place. But God's plans were being accomplished. He was working in a powerful way to provide salvation and eternal life for all who trust in Jesus.

Immediately at Jesus' death, the curtain in the house of God was torn in two from top to bottom. The earth shook, and big rocks split in two. Graves were opened, and the bodies of many of God's people who were dead were raised to life! The captain of the soldiers and those with him who were watching Jesus saw all the things that were happening. They saw the earth shake, and they were terrified. They said, "For sure, this Man really was the Son of God."

And this Man is the one who saves you from sin when you believe in Him. Have you asked Jesus to forgive your sins and change your life?

(Adapted from Matthew 27)

DECEMBER

Prayers by and about Jesus

As you enjoy the Christmas season this year, think about Jesus in every fun activity. His birth is the reason we celebrate! As you're decorating the house and putting up the tree, think about Jesus—how beautiful and amazing He is! When you're exchanging gifts, think about Jesus—remember all gifts are from Him and in honor of Him. As you're making cookies and candy and enjoying a great big feast, think about Jesus—thank Him for all the yummy food to eat. As you're playing Christmas songs and games, think about Jesus—worship Him for being *Immanuel*, God with us. When you're helping and donating to others, think about Jesus—remember that anything you do for others in need is like serving Jesus Himself. Keep your thoughts on Him, and let all your prayers be filled with knowledge and wonder of Him. The Bible teaches us so much about Jesus, and we learn even from the prayers that He prayed and that others prayed about Him. Read the following stories this month and see for yourself!

"MY EYES HAVE SEEN THE CHOSEN ONE"

Simeon's Prayer about Jesus

An old man named Simeon lived in Jerusalem at the time Jesus was born. Simeon was a good man who loved the one true God and was eagerly looking for the time when God would send the promised Savior to rescue His people. The Holy Spirit had told Simeon that he would not die before he had seen God's Chosen One.

One special day, the Holy Spirit led Simeon to be at the temple. It was the same day Mary and Joseph brought baby Jesus to present Him to God. According to the Jewish law, parents were to give a gift of two young birds on the altar in worship to the Lord.

When Simeon saw baby Jesus at the temple, he was thrilled! God's promise to him had come true. He was finally seeing the Chosen One! Simeon took baby Jesus in his arms. Then he gave honor and thanks to God, saying, "Lord, now let me die in peace, as You have said. My eyes have seen the Chosen One who will save men from the punishment of their sins. You have made Him ready in the sight of all nations. He will be a light to shine on all people."

Joseph and Mary were surprised and wondered about what Simeon had said. Simeon honored and blessed them and said to Mary, the mother of Jesus, "See! This Child will make many people fall and many people rise in the Jewish nation. He will be spoken against and opposed. And a sword will cut through your soul." Simeon was saying that people would either love or reject Jesus, and Mary would be very sad over the way Jesus would be hated by many.

When Joseph and Mary finished what they'd come to do, they left Jerusalem and took baby Jesus back to Nazareth in Galilee. And Jesus grew and became strong in spirit. He was filled with wisdom and the loving-favor of God.

Unlike Simeon, you've never actually seen or touched Jesus. But you know Him through God's Word, the Bible. Pray to know Jesus more and more—someday you *will* see Him face-to-face!

(Adapted from Luke 2)

"OUR FATHER IN HEAVEN, YOUR NAME IS HOLY"

Jesus' Teaching about How to Pray

Jesus taught in many places while He lived on earth. One day He went up on a mountainside and began to teach about many things to the people who gathered and listened. This was His "Sermon on the Mount." He taught about loving our enemies and giving to the needy. He taught about not worrying and about building up treasure in heaven. He taught about false prophets and a wise builder. He taught about all of that and much more!

Jesus also taught people how to pray. He said, "When you pray, do not be like those people who pretend to be someone they're not. They love to stand and pray where people can see them. Surely, I tell you, they have all the reward they are going to get." He went on, "When you pray, go into a room alone and pray to your Father in secret. Then your Father will reward you. When you pray, do not say the same thing over and over again, making long prayers like the people who do not know God. They think they are heard because their prayers are long. Don't be like them. Your Father knows what you need before you ask Him."

Then Jesus gave us a way to pray. He said, "Pray like this: 'Our Father in heaven, Your name is holy. May Your holy nation come. May what You want done on earth be done as it is in heaven. Give us the bread we need today. Forgive us our sins as we forgive those who sin against us. Do not let us be tempted, but keep us from sin. Your nation is holy. You have power and shining-greatness forever.'"

Jesus didn't mean this is the only prayer we should ever pray. He gave us an example of prayer that we can use to create our own prayers. In all our prayers, we should be sincere and know that God is perfectly holy. We should pray for God's kingdom to come and for His will to be done. We should ask for our daily needs to be met. We should ask for forgiveness for ourselves and for the ability to forgive others. We should ask for help not to sin, and we should praise God. Jesus was so good to teach us this way to pray!

(Adapted from Matthew 6)

"FATHER, HONOR YOUR NAME!"
Jesus' Prayer for God's Glory

Jesus visited His friends Mary, Martha, and Lazarus during the last days before His death on the cross. They made Him supper, and then Mary took a jar of expensive perfume and poured it out on Jesus' feet. Then she dried His feet with her hair. The wonderful smell of the special perfume filled the house. Mary was showing her great love and honor for Jesus.

The next day, many people in Jerusalem heard Jesus was coming, and they were excited to welcome Him. They took palm branches and went to meet Him. They shouted in praise, "Hosanna! Greatest One! Great and honored is He who comes in the name of the Lord, the King of the Jews!" Jesus found a young donkey and sat on it. A prophet named Zechariah had predicted that hundreds of years earlier. He had written, "Do not be afraid, people of Jerusalem. See! Your King comes sitting on a young donkey!"

The people who had been with Jesus when He had called Lazarus from the grave kept telling others about that incredible miracle. They had seen Lazarus raised from the dead! That's why many people wanted to meet Jesus. But the proud religious law keepers were upset that Jesus was there and said among themselves, "Look, we are losing followers. Everyone is following Jesus!"

Jesus said to the people, "The hour is near for the Son of Man to be taken to heaven to receive great honor. Surely, I tell you, unless a seed falls into the ground and dies, it will only be a seed. If it dies, it will give much grain. Anyone who loves their life will lose it. Anyone who hates their life in this world will keep it forever. Anyone who wants to serve Me must follow Me. And My Father will honor anyone who serves Me."

Then Jesus, knowing He would soon suffer and die, said, "Now My soul is troubled. Should I say, 'Father, save Me from this time of trouble and pain'? No, for this is why I came to this time. So, Father, honor Your name!"

Jesus knew God's plan for Him would not be easy. In fact, it would be terrible. But Jesus also knew that God was working out His perfect plan of salvation. Jesus was willing to do whatever His Father told Him. More than anything, Jesus wanted to bring glory to God.

That is our greatest job too. Today, ask God how you can bring Him glory. He'll be happy to answer that prayer.

(Adapted from Zechariah 9; John 12)

"I THANK YOU, FATHER"
Jesus' Prayer of Gratitude

Jesus sent out seventy of His followers, two by two, to the places He would visit and teach in next. He said to them, "There is much grain ready to gather. But the workmen are few. Pray then that the Lord, who owns the grain fields, will send workmen to gather His grain." Jesus meant there were many people who needed to hear about Him and believe.

He said to the followers He sent out, "Go on your way. Listen! I send you out like lambs among wolves. Take no money. Speak to no one along the way. When you go into a house, say that you hope peace will come to them. If your good wishes are not received, they will come back to you."

He continued, "Whenever a city welcomes you, eat the things that are put before you there. Heal the sick. Say to them, 'The holy nation of God is near.' Whatever city does not welcome you, go into its streets and say, 'Know that the holy nation of God has come near you!' I tell you, on the day men stand before God, things will not be easy for that city."

And Jesus said, "Whoever listens to you listens to Me. Whoever has nothing to do with you has nothing to do with Me. Whoever has nothing to do with Me has nothing to do with God, who sent Me."

When the seventy people Jesus had sent out came back, they were full of joy over what Jesus had given them the power to do. They said, "Lord, even the demons obeyed us when we used Your name."

Jesus said to them, "I saw Satan fall from heaven like lightning. Listen! I have given you power to walk on snakes and trample scorpions. I have given you power to defeat the enemy. Nothing will hurt you. Even so, you should not be happy because the demons obey you. Instead, be happy because your names are written in heaven."

And then Jesus was filled with the joy of the Holy Spirit. He said, "I thank You, Father, Lord of heaven and earth. You have shown these things to little children. Yes, Father, it was what You wanted done."

Jesus was grateful to God the Father that eternal life is available to anyone who comes to Him like a little child.

(Adapted from Luke 10)

A YEAR TO CELEBRATE!

New Year's Day
January 1
New Year's Day is the first day of the new year. It's a holiday that helps us look ahead with hope to the coming year.

Martin Luther King Jr. Day
Third Monday in January
Martin Luther King Jr. Day is celebrated near the birthday of Martin Luther King Jr., who was born on January 15, 1929. Martin Luther King Jr. is known and celebrated for his life's work of spreading kindness, fairness, and racial equality among all people.

Valentine's Day
February 14
Valentine's Day is a special day to celebrate and promote love. People give each other cards and gifts and flowers, and many couples celebrate with special dinners too.

Presidents' Day
Third Monday in February
Presidents' Day especially honors two important presidents of the United States of America, George Washington and Abraham Lincoln. It also celebrates all American presidents. It is held near the birthday of the first American president, George Washington, who was born on February 22, 1732.

Saint Patrick's Day
March 17
Saint Patrick's Day is a special day to celebrate Irish traditions because of Saint Patrick, who was a Christian saint remembered and honored for helping to bring Christianity to Ireland.

Ash Wednesday
February or March
Ash Wednesday is the first day of Lent, which is forty days (not including Sundays) of fasting and turning from our sins before the celebration of Easter.

Palm Sunday
The Sunday before Easter
Palm Sunday remembers the day Jesus Christ arrived in Jerusalem on a donkey. The people cut palm branches and laid them in the road for His donkey to walk on while they welcomed and praised Him.

Good Friday
The Friday before Easter
Good Friday remembers the day Jesus Christ was arrested and put to death on the cross to take the punishment for sin and save all who believe in Him.

Easter
A Sunday in March or April
Easter celebrates that Jesus Christ rose to life again after death and that He offers eternal life to all who trust in Him as Savior.

National Day of Prayer
First Thursday in May
The National Day of Prayer is a special day in the United States of America for encouraging people to turn to God in prayer.

Mother's Day
Second Sunday in May
Mother's Day is a special day to remember, honor, and appreciate mothers for their hard work and love in raising their children.

Memorial Day
Last Monday in May
Memorial Day remembers and honors those who have died serving in the military of the United States of America.

Flag Day
June 14
Flag Day remembers when leaders first established a flag to represent the United States of America, during the Revolutionary War, on June 14, 1777.

Father's Day
Third Sunday in June
Father's Day is a special day to remember, honor, and appreciate fathers for their hard work and love in raising their children.

Independence Day
July 4
The Fourth of July honors the day the United States of America declared itself an independent nation and adopted the written Declaration of Independence. Picnics and fireworks are popular ways to celebrate.

Labor Day
First Monday in September
Labor Day is a special day to celebrate American workers.

Veterans Day
November 11
Veterans Day honors all who have served in the armed forces of the United States.

Thanksgiving Day
Fourth Thursday in November
Thanksgiving is a special day to celebrate and give thanks for all things God has given. It's a time for gathering with family and friends and enjoying a feast together.

Christmas Day
December 25
Christmas is the special day to remember and honor the birth of Jesus Christ. People exchange gifts and have many special traditions, foods, and feasts with family and friends to celebrate the season.

MY NOTES

MY NOTES

MY NOTES

....

....

....

....

....

....

....

....

....

....

....

....

....

SKETCH PAGE

If You Enjoyed *A Year of Bible Prayers,*
DON'T MISS *A YEAR OF BIBLE STORIES!*

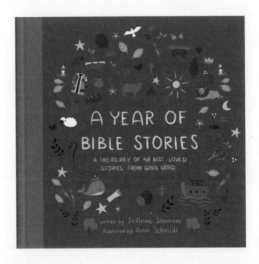

A Year of Bible Stories is sure to become a story-time favorite in your house! This lovely keepsake Bible storybook for kids celebrates each month of the calendar year with 48 best-loved stories from God's Word. Each colorfully illustrated story reinforces the monthly theme and shows kids how God worked in the lives of Bible men and women—and how He works in the lives of people today!

Hardcover / ISBN 978-1-64352-640-9